Door to Remain

Door to Remain

Austin Segrest

WINNER 2021 VASSAR MILLER PRIZE IN POETRY

UNIVERSITY OF NORTH TEXAS PRESS

DENTON, TEXAS

10 9 8 7 6 5 4 3 2 1

Permissions:
University of North Texas Press
1155 Union Circle #311336
Denton, TX 76203-5017

The paper used in this book meets the minimum requirements of the American
National Standard for Permanence of Paper for Printed Library Materials, z39.48.1984.
Binding materials have been chosen for durability.

Names: Segrest, Austin, author.
Title: Door to remain / Austin Segrest.
Other titles: Vassar Miller prize in poetry series ; no. 29.
Description: Denton, TX : University of North Texas Press, [2022] | Series:
    Number 29 in the Vassar Miller Poetry Prize series
Identifiers: LCCN 2021052455 (print) | LCCN 2021052456 (ebook) | ISBN
    9781574418644 (paperback) | ISBN 9781574418750 (ebook)
Subjects: LCSH: Mothers and sons--Poetry. | Southern States--Poetry. |
    LCGFT: Elegies (Poetry)
Classification: LCC PS3619.E378 D66 2022 (print) | LCC PS3619.E378
    (ebook) | DDC 811/.6--dc23/eng/20211105
LC record available at https://lccn.loc.gov/2021052455
LC ebook record available at https://lccn.loc.gov/2021052456

Door to Remain is Number 29 in the Vassar Miller Poetry Prize Series

The electronic edition of this book was made possible by
the support of the Vick Family Foundation.

Cover and text design by Sarah Schulte

for Susu and Broki,
April's fools

April doet wat hij wil

CONTENTS

II.

III.

For woe to us, so greate a Breach when was

John Fiske

Meet the Beatles

after John Murillo

Just what that something is   the "Oh yeah, you"
John says she's got   the hand he wants to hold
and which part of love   because he can, he must
he hides with his guitar   the kind of man
he begs to be   the words inside her mouth
when my mother set the needle   rooting down
into the raunch   to beat time out of need
there wasn't a one of her girlfriends   "Oh yeah, you"
clapping, bangs, hips   the syncopated drums
who didn't come at once to understand
her record player and books and piles of records
the hand he wants to hold   when my mother
set the needle and on cue   with the strum
the words inside her mouth   began to rhyme
there wasn't a one of her girlfriends gathered round
to hear the news   her long frame rooting down
into the raunch where rock and roll began
with the first "Oh yeah, you"   that happiness
he hides with his guitar   there wasn't a one
of her girlfriends gathered round her record player
and books and piles of records   who didn't come
when he begs to be her man   to rhyme her body
with the strum   the double backbeat drums
to understand   just what that something is
John says she's got   the kind of man he means
clapping, bangs, hips   where rock and roll began
to beat time out of need   need out of time

I.

Across the Street

I ran across the street, I didn't know any better.
Ran out in the street, I didn't know no better.
I just knew a woman was there, though I'd never met her.

She sat me in her parlor, distracted me with trinkets,
milky glass birds and fish, distracting trinkets.
She said my mother would be fine, but did she think it?

The world was a blur of crystal wings and fins.
My tears were casked in crystal, wings and fins.
She was the first of many lady-friends.

The tree shadows shortened, she brought me a drink of water.
Morning matured, she brought me a glass of water.
I drank it so fast, she went and brought another.

I kept looking out the window, she didn't ask me what for.
I watched out that window, she didn't ask what for.
The seconds broke off and lay there on the floor.

I imagined my mother's route, as far as I could.
Her long morning walk, followed as far as I could.
Nothing I could do would do any good.

Suffer the little children, and forbid them not.
Christ said suffer the little children, and forbid them not.
Said love thy neighbor, sometimes she's all you got.

Cahaba Heights

Mom parks us at the window.
My brother holds onto the stroller,
as he, and my sister and I inside it,
watch sheep graze across the street,
waiting for the black one.

In its fishbowl glass bottle red wine
wobbles under a picture of a castle.

Clouds of hair with cheeks like powdered doughnuts
crowd the stroller, smelling like flowers.
One digs her rings in my curls and sings
what she wouldn't give for those lashes.
I grin and bat them.

I grin and batten
on the milk of their laughter.

Preamble

I got up in time to see her hand weights windmill
over the hill. No telling how long it would take,
if she'd be back. My brother moaned, *she's fine*.
My sister humored the possibility
with a little frown, then suggested we toast paper sandwiches
under her desk lamp, or play the game where one of us
scribbles with closed eyes, then the other adapts
the scribble to look like something that in some dimension
might be alive. My heart hammered out the world
once seen as one, as if it were being read to the three of us,
hammered out all thoughts but one. It got light.
I watched the slope of Dover,
uncrested by her.
                    Only once, on her birthday,
I thought to come along. April Fool's Day.
From out of the depths, for the first time, the color
of the new sky struck me. It was warm already.
Redbuds and azaleas made neat pastel incisions,
at the same time anesthetizing the patient with their fragrance,
balsam and balm, a running froth of blossom
acute against the impracticable blue,
against her vanishing.

Shades Creek, Panther Sighting

All the way to the doctor I kept watch,
not saying anything. When she went in
(I knew it was about her unhappiness),
I stood outside the handsome doctor's door
at the end of a narrow hallway looking out
the south wall of windows where a creek
flashed in the thicket, a bend of sand.
I imagined its ragged breathing, visible,
though it was summer, in the damp
of some ravine. The lavender carpet
had faded in the sun. There was a painting
(a soupy abstract), a potted tree,
and I was a bird perched there, listening.
The silence outside the door was enormous.
She'd said, sure, go play in the creek, seeing
that I was thinking there might be tracks.
I said I would but stayed there by the door,
mortified, red splotches printing my neck.
Mostly clay, the sand turned red. The creek
turned back beneath the street and ran
on in my mind, under the waterwheel,
a slit between fairways hardly noticed
tamped-down gray school mornings
getting whipped around those hills,
houses jutting and rolling along the ridge.

My Mother's Morning Walks

She took her turn around the house—
unreachable circumference.

She dropped below a hundred pounds,
a snail shell with the back blown out.

The shell's eye whorled around the house.
A roundhouse horse that walked her course

that circumscribed my universe,
she took a turn for the worse.

The axle's force that turned the stars
unharnessed from the horse.

The Alabama Theater

Over Big Bertha, Birmingham's Wurlitzer,
worth more than the ornate, smoke-stained building
it was a kind of tiered model of, my mother

read me the title cards I was too young for.
I tried to follow behind the mirror where the phantom
took the girl—behind the mask, behind the cards

and silence, beneath the Paris Opera House
and the production of *Faust*, to where the phantom,
the Spirit of Music, like the haint left in the house

at the end of *Absalom, Absalom!*, played the organ.
I understood she was divided, an understudy.
That she had no choice between men, between marriage

and a career, an inner darkness
that would never leave her, and a white veneer.
On the other side of me, my father explained

how the phantom could breathe through his reed
in the secret waters of the Seine.
We were looking in a mirror, a crowd watching a crowd

in the show watch a show in a silent movie
from sixty years before, when downtown wasn't dead,
but zoned, and the new movie palace brought vaudeville

and pageants and the silent flick to a people
desperate among the faux opera trappings not to feel
common. After the empires and opera,

but before the Depression and television
and the flight of tax dollars and highways, they listened
to the same four-manual organ and saw themselves

in the mob at the end chasing the phantom
like a janitor out of the cellar with torches.
"Feast your eyes—glut your soul!" my mother whispered.

Doormat

The part of the dream I forgot was running from bed,
and, pausing to hope it would work, diving inside,
as if translated into the world that I could see
but couldn't read through her glass paperweight.

Pausing to hope it would work, I dove through the mat.
Floating down a wide well, I searched through caverns, or crypts,
but couldn't read through her cut-glass paperweight.
She hadn't died yet, but I knew she was promised.

Floating down a wide well, I searched through caverns.
Donne says batter my heart, I've done him one better.
She'd live twenty more years, but I knew she was promised.
I've battered my head against the door, against the bed.

Donne says batter my heart. I've done him one better.
Against bodies and other heads, against the pomegranate
I've battered my head. Against the door, against the bed.
Seven seeds was all she ate. The door was shut, the bolt was thrown.

Against bodies and other heads, against the pomegranate:
how do you knock when what's asked of you is only
seven seeds—all she would eat. The door was shut, the bolt was thrown.
The reason a riddle no child could answer.

How do you ask when what's asked of you is only
what you least want to give? The secret of beauty is death.
The reason's a riddle that even a child could answer,
a secret on which only a mother could let you in.

The Shirelles

The already redundant   "Everybody
Loves a Lover"   the raw hopscotch caprice
crowding close and backing away   the horns
and drums muffled, in another room   the "you
you-you" of all that's lost   my mother looped
on the end of her lullaby   a girl again
as an ear trumpet extends   the ever extending
ever deafening ear   what's remembered
gets magnified   my mother at the end
lost in double-time   the "you, you-you"
I never knew   extended "since I fell in love with you"
the spun honey   of songwriters crammed
two-to-a-cubicle in the Brill Building
with just a piano and a chair   the first you
syncopated   then two in double-time
I strained through tubed ears to hear   sick
for each you strung over the raw hum and static
like an old vet leaning   with his ear trumpet
the first you extending   gets magnified
that trinity love   is ever in excess of
lost on me   until after she died
syncopated   muffled, in another room

Cold Sweat

When my mother danced alone
to Wilson Pickett's caterwaul

we were snowbound in New York
drinking whiskey to stay warm.

Her shimmy baited the candles
from their wicks, and I burned

like I'd been left out in the snow.
My aunt clapped from her chair,

my uncle smiled across the den
as if to say it wasn't what it seemed.

I called her *drunk* and *ugly*
because she meant everything,

every rock and swivel of her hips.

Gum

The gum she bought by the flat. Blue or green,
mixed in her mouth with the brown chaw we found
in its pouch in the drawer, it congealed—
kneaded and jowled, wrung-out as a fear,
a grief, a grudge—into amorphous gray.

Like a rock, until you touched it.
Asking about it was futile. It was her gum.
How come she saved it? To chew again.
How come it was gray?… I know our questions
felt like accusations, though we hardly knew

what chewing tobacco was. Eventually,
older kids in the neighborhood were consulted.
But since the unholy combination was otherwise
unheard of, it was a working theory,
theoretically suspended like the tobacco juice

we couldn't but figure she swallowed.
Combining, saving, savoring—what could be worth
such gruesome thrift? You found yourself
staring at it, thinking of it as an asteroid
escaped from one of Dad's always incompatible

books across the hall. Or when I was sure, again,
something had happened to her, and lay on her side
of the bed looking at it in its ashen, abandoned
disfigurement, as if there—unlike in the words
on the page where I was afraid of getting lost,

of screaming and screaming and no one
could hear—; as if there I could read,
by the light of love's forensics, all
that she swallowed, all that went unsaid,
the marks of a seal, a worked-over, hallowed terrain.

In the Check-Out

Hushed into depths beyond the watcher's diving
Byron

Like a long-bored or long-defunct
charity-case bodyguard taking up
his accustomed distractions,

too discerning, but only just, for the tabloids,
too impatient for fiction, I occupied myself,
while Mom got groceries,

with true crime and unsolved mysteries—
Kids Who Kill, a man walks out in his field
and vanishes. Or I'd peruse

the rotary display case of watches:
strap fashions, moon-phase displays,
and other complications

brought to heel around the dial—
the farmer's rusty sickle taught the tune
of an oscillating crystal.

Enrichment

I twist the bright yarns twined up my skinny arms
like Swatch watches or Viking bands, as if by sheer
accrual I can measure up. Weren't they called
friendship bracelets? The Test Administrator
has no face I can remember. Even as I'm charmed,
I distrust his measured encouragement
about the situation with the fulcrum (which he explains
away) and the string of numbers he wants to see
if I can repeat, and then, why not, repeat them backwards,
and other puzzles he pretends I'm equal to,
even as he notes that I am not, notes the sham,
the shame no ornament can hide: that I do not
particularly excel at solving problems,
but only, it would seem, at causing them,
and that my fate will be to only marginally contribute
to future profits, and that if I am gifted,
it's with gifts I've given myself, or found, or stolen,
and woven about me like a magpie, or a prophet.

Vestavia

Come summer I'd let her go
shopping alone. I'd start smoking.

I'd start working at the tennis shoe
megastore, selling shoes

under the strobe and throb
of mid-nineties pomp. I'd steal.

Get caught. Before I began
to humiliate her at every turn

in return for being humiliated,
I accompanied my mother

to run errands, as she called it.
There's this stretch of Highway 31

that climbs a hill south of town,
one of those places I come to

realize I'm seeing while thinking
of something else entirely. And it was here,

having come along for errands,
my loathing of which was almost

equal to the fear of losing her,
my need to keep her near, alive—

the balance nearly struck; it was here
among unraveling flag-lined

intersections, used car lots, the advent
of the strip mall, a Sears, the first

Subway in town; here, below
a little gazebo temple to Vesta

overlooking her shitty province
of stoplights (goddess, I knew,

of the hearth, but not what a hearth was);
it was here, entrenched in the backseat,

enraged I didn't know why, that I
refused a haircut, opting instead

to stay in the hot car. That I wasn't
ashamed anymore of my curls,

at least not enough to join in
the awful commerce of Vestavia,

which ate up so much life, her life,
that had become so much her life—

seemed both to hurt and please her.
I couldn't have said which

I wanted more. Watching me
in the rearview watch that temple,

little more, I knew, than a prop,
she said, "You really are my *David*,"

—and left me to imagine what I slew.

Wyeth

The Helga Pictures, 1987

In the front room of my adolescence,
on a dresser of blond wood beneath a mirror

facing the front door nobody much used,
Helga caught the barnlight in her red hair.

Cover to cover, one day she appeared.
If they noticed at all, nobody mentioned It.

Southfacing, walled with picture windows
like a greenhouse, it wasn't a room, really,

but an open concept for the Alabama sun,
its every last syllable and squib.

The pale carpet warm even in winter,
I stood with my back to the light

and turned the golden pages of Helga's
plaited hair, lost in the lines and shadows

of her unpainted, sunpainted skin:
Wyeth's secret, nude,

but no nubile muse.
The rubbertree dropped its gum on the carpet.

The sun sat up straight at the table,
in the never-used loveseat and chairs,

which, freed from the concepts of living
or dining, commenced slowly to fade,

as I turned the barnlight over, looking for Helga
on the porch, the hair above her unpainted lip

glistening in profile. I didn't know whether
to abscond with the book to the bathroom

or stay suspended in wonder at how close
I had to look to see that it was painted,

planted in that world of faded barns.

Our Lady of Sorrows

There were the Scalisis and the Troncollis…
St. Christopher, protector
of something or other,
hung from Paul's neck,
watching as Paul did not
as I snuck answers from his sheet.
What made a Catholic Catholic?
A church across from one of the libraries
Mom would dog was called Our Lady of Sorrows.
I was a reluctant reader,
but they couldn't keep enough
books on the shelves for Mom and my sister,
who would have been at home,
in her own world, waiting
for new books. I was starting
to suffer from acute boredom,
a species of fear. Mom set me up
with an oversize book on aircraft carriers
and car magazines they were getting rid of
for a dime and disappeared
among the stacks. The big study tables,
the circulation desk more of a deck,
the oaken card catalogue with its brass fittings
and narrow, heavy drawers like the stops
of an ancient instrument I was
too intimidated to learn,
and which a forebear in some Swiss canton
might have smashed once to spars—
all smelling faintly of Pine-Sol.
Low ceilings and lights, like school,
but not. The intimate anonymity
of strangers slowed in their musings.
Exposed in the churchyard, a bright white Mary's
features were indistinct.

We tried coming up with all seven sorrows.
A tall glass prow housed the cathedral
and a school. What was the difference
between a parish and a church?
What *was* clear was who *our* lady was—
that tears had turned Lot's wife to salt.
As bedtime rolled around, spending the night
at a friend's, panic would set in,
like a pen scratching out an answer
till it tears through the page.
Wall phone in its cradle, the deep
sloping yard blacked out below
our reflection in the kitchen windows,
Mrs. Murray, in her white nightgown,
assured me angels were guarding her house.
I'd never heard an adult say something like that
and took it as a sign that she was touched.
Our church was easy to miss
below the road, and it was hard to tell
where the front was, like it kept
its back to you—stones
that covered Stephen, wood
that hid the deed. Down-to-earth,
though not without grandeur,
it was neither the oldest nor most exclusive
Episcopal house of worship. Plus,
Mom had it bad for the priest.
It's arguable we experienced more
communion and certainly as much
ritual at the House of Pancakes.
The only sermon I remember,
because it was so frightening,
was something to the effect of
what if you walked in the kitchen
one night and God was in there?
Compared to that, Dad's absence

felt as arbitrary as a stanza break.
Only once more would Mom and my brother
and sister and I sit in a pew.
Down the hill from the first house
she rented after the divorce, it wasn't
Universalist, like I thought,
but Anglican, which figures. Candlelit,
pungent with boughs and holly,
the nave had a steep-pitched roof
that reached to the ground, except
for a line of windows where she squeezed us in.
Midnight mass, I guess.
We didn't know what else to do
but sing. At least we knew the songs.
A full house, strangers' voices swept us up
over the golf course, off the ridge,
and stole our stomachs diving into Jones Valley.
Mom was crying, it was all a little crazy.
Then my sister. All the Christmas lights,
doubled in all the glass, were crossed
by headlights sweeping past on Montevallo.

Montevallo

One suitor, one plain robin of a man
came down the walk to the front door,
slender, bald, too neat. And after that,
Mom hung it up. At fifty,
she'd just returned to work and being single.

Around that time, in the middle of a spat
I don't remember about what, three teens
under her roof, I leveled
my unconscious compulsion, the air gun,
at a bird in the driveway. If the sky
was the unimpeachable blue of its eggs,
I wasn't paying attention. I wasn't thinking
of the blue jay's bloody raids she used to cry
telling us about. I wasn't thinking *robin*,
just *moving target*.
                    Not that it moved.
It was like putting the gun against the screen
in *Duck Hunt*. The worst part was, everyone—
my brother, sister, and mom—stopped fighting
to watch. Like they were lining up the sights,
or lined up in them.

                    We were so vulnerable!
In the sudden quiet, the robin fell
without protest. And with the gasps
and groans and looks of uncomprehending horror,
our pain was sublimated, rearranged.
Polar and nonpolar, water and oil,
and between us a bond, a bridge, a barrel.

The Chance for a Simple Act

Dear Friends, there are moments when
we have the chance for a simple act
Joseph Stroud

In the crowded subway station I reached down
and lifted the front of the stroller,
exchanging smiles with the mother

but no words as I recall as we lifted the stroller
up the flight of stairs she'd been corralled
to the foot of. At the top we put it down,

she thanked me, and my friend,
who was walking ahead of me, turned and said
I was a good person. Though there were hardly

forty years between the two of us, my friend
didn't take everything for granted like me,
to whom, cameraless that summer, she gave

her doubles and cast-offs: blurry statues, a coastline.
But this memory I captured from the swarm,
from the New York City exodus of impressions:

reaching down without thinking, my friend
turning to tell me I was good. I think of this
more than I should, probably, if it were true,

when I remember how cruelly I treated my mother
before she died, denying her younger friends
at work were her real friends. And my friend,

26

Krisi, if she thinks of me at all and all
she gave me—the love we made and the love
that I withheld—maybe she thinks of it, too.

Where She Walked

Up and down the ridge on streets
that worked around outcroppings and creeks.
Out of every outfit
clean through the closet,
a candle boiled down
to a rich and piercing clarity.
Into her most private reserves,
before the sun slipped out,
while we slept.
Down to her maternal
mitochondria's spattering altars,
with herself to herself,
her own ambergris and oil,
the present outpacing the past,
every pink revolution and solemn fast,
feasting on that prolonged deferral
of the first bite, the will.

II.

Majestic Diner

ATLANTA, GA

> My God, what is a heart?
> *George Herbert*

♦

This far east it was a different town
when they'd ride out for milkshakes in the '50s.
Charmingly rundown now, the businesses
(not a few, brunch spots) snaking down the hill
were ripe for developing. A City Hall
famed for squat square footage was already
a designer mall in someone's mind.

♦

Freedom Parkway's redbuds had just gone off,
with the pears lining Ponce de Leon,
which Mom still called Poncey, close behind.
We were beginning in that new millennium
to ease into a friendship as fragile
as my early-twenties hangover
(what is it to be southern, anyway,
but to trust in the salve, the grace of grease?).
Out here, for an afternoon and a few
others like it, she ate what she wanted.

◆

We hadn't been so free with each other
since I was very young, like old friends
reuniting. She was open about smoking—
a little—again. About her attraction
to the owner, a man with meat on him
and gold chains in his chest hair, whose son
had OD'd. I let go and told her
how though the girl I loved had moved
I saw her everywhere. The pain of thinking
that we didn't have a chance resolved
in the mutual call of appetite,
abandoning our bodies to the breaking
of the pancakes' lacey edge together.

♦

We were only down the road
but were as far as we could get
from her apartment,
its unassuming brick
a postwar affair
made when she was,
and which we shared
miserably that year,
her last. I was just starting
to move out. She liked that the ceilings,
at least, were high,
high enough, anyway,
not to embarrass her
cast-off inheritance
of heavy furniture,
wingbacks and dressers,
a dining room table and chairs
and sideboard missing a leg
she called with high-church flair
a credenza—broken cupboard
of her mother's faith,
her father's credit:
wood she hated but wanted,
like her body, a certain way.
Every old stick of which
I'd moved returned us
to a past we never intended
to revisit—or to visit
on each other, a rehearsal
of ruin worked out in food:

her mother's prowess,
my father's about-face
in 1980 or so, when grease
proved a culprit
in heart disease.
Still, she persisted
fixing me the quick,
filling suppers of my youth,
balanced on the tooth
of my ingratitude. Late,
alone, she ate
her pile of roasted cabbage
and blackened Brussels
doused in soy sauce
and read and did not want
to be disturbed.
That she had trouble
swallowing, as much
as she'd admit.

♦

Old or new, white money
was back—or wanted to be
taken back, abusive husband,
having fled in the '60s (when Mom
went off to college), like her dad
coming back from Florida to remarry
her mom on her deathbed. Waltzing in
like it owned the place, it would be made
to wait.

♦

Out here, we could get out
from under each other:
corporate margin
almost New Orleans
in its mild air
of age and license.
Little seam of Ponce,
in French, of *thought*
she could have quipped,
a *going all along,*
a little room,
a little Rome.

♦

On a Post-It over the sink
was once written "Think
@ 10 am" in her immaculate
hand. It meant
to remember each other,
like a ring's reminder
to a single mother
and her three disbanded teens.
This was in the house
on Montevallo,
her first. A mindless,
overqualified hour
into some shit job,
the printer, the pizza parlor,
a moment saved,
a little ceremony,
like a midmorning smoke
or a sip of water
between classes.

♦

The spring teased
and nudged us out,
like being introduced
to her 90-year-old neighbor—
Milton, was it? His was the first
unit off the slightly musty,
worn-carpeted hall
(hers was at the end
on the right). He came to the door
like he'd been waiting
and took my hand,
a prospectless,
begrudging scrub
living with his mother after college.
His eyes shone
at the gates of bone,
so lucid I couldn't look away,
so even I could see
he liked what he saw:
that he could espouse
how she must be so proud,
how handsome I was.

◆

Everything was agreeable:
the weather, the bacon, our waiter.
Almost pretty in all black,
there was something a touch—
touchingly—melancholic
about his East Atlanta mystique
that you'd call hipster now,
where emo met rockabilly's
ragged edge. He reminded Mom,
of all things, of Michael Jackson
in—what else?

♦

Remnant of Little Richard, blur
of James Brown's loafers,
spark from her disco days.
Glitter, and curl, and wind—
she loved to watch him dance,
his face-lift taunting her
that she was *outta time*
while he was *outside* of it:
'50s Michael we needn't be told
isn't like other guys,
'80s Michael in that amazing vented red
patent leather jacket with the ribbed
shoulders and black tunic V
a new kid showed up in in Kindergarten,
his name a shape no one could guess
(not Circle or Heart or Square)
before he made his entrance.
Time the *creature creeping up behind*,
like a father or a brother or an uncle
reprised in a son. Green Michael,
grave Michael, death's-head Michael
calling from within, or crawling out
of Oakland Cemetery's jumbled vaults
after the tornado desegregated them.

◆

It made no sense, he was white.
But why not?
Like a holidaying parent (when in Rome),
I let her have it, I let it slide
down our throats.
Maybe the cheekbones, I told myself,
maybe the frame.

♦

Conquistador or revolutionary
from the pages of history,
thirty-years-ago-drawn
with fabric crayons
and brought home for Mom
to sew onto this cushion, his hair coiffed
into a helmet, his brown skin
and nose showing signs of revision,
his epaulets like cupcakes on his shoulders,
there is
no telling who he was
supposed to be.

But she would always see
the King of Pop—or Pomp—
in his sequined Grammys
marching band getup.

◆

What is an icon
but a likeness?

♦

Behind us, a cook was starting shit,
or finishing it,
laying into our little Thriller
hell-for-leather.
Backed against the wall,
he flinched and wilted to the tall
cook's delight.
Did she see it?
In my mind I hide it from her,
but in truth I can't remember.
The padded kitchen door
swung shut. I could see him
crying through the diamond.

♦

In an old nightmare, burnt black
in a crash, it was Mom's thumb
on a cushion our maid's Black hands
offered up.

◆

Our waiter
was only *wearing* black.

♦

His was a kind
of misfit performance
she delighted in,
even while condemning it
in my friends.

As if she were trying
to keep me off the scent
of what she felt
she really was.

To have done
what was done.

♦

She'd have sympathized
with Michael's twisted proclivities,
twisted up in a childhood, which,
like hers, never existed.

So she insisted
on playing the witch
in that same classroom.
Under the cover of darkness serving up
fruit punch to the little goblins
and princesses and superheroes,
her cauldron steaming
with dry ice we had to drive
to a factory on the Black
Northside of Birmingham to buy.

♦

And if, like Michael's gleaming suit
on the cover, in some sense,
she saw all servers as Black,
as servants?

She served me my whole life.

♦

Michael's hair, larded and flammable,
his blood-red jacket threatening
to turn into a sports car at any moment,
his child voice incommensurate
with his sadistic glee,
cup after cup of thin coffee
and the rarity of really eating with her,
a fortune made by starving
a large one, Love's conquistadors
and victims, his rejects and stars:
sup with us, forgive us, we ate,
we ate our hearts out, as Love wept.

III.

She Went In and Out

of the world with America
dropping bombs.
Bombing was her birthright.
Decisive expedient incontrovertible,
the bombs saved
staved shaved
the hour.

Boomer, she lived
fifty-nine years
in holy terror,
canned goods,
frozen Beef 'n Cheddars,
a pile of candy bars
stationed on her kitchen
island like airmen
bored in the Caribbean,
fat men, little boys,
waiting for the end.

When I said we had no business
invading the one time
we strayed into politics,
she said, sheepishly,
but 9/11. It was spring.
The bombs were falling.

The Monkey

It's not any species I can find.
It has a white beard and grayish hair
with a widow's peak that seems to continue
dark gray down its nose and around
its white-lipped smile.
Sitting at the edge of a murky forest,
its body is smooth and brown.
It holds a red peach in one hand,
its tail draped in the other
like a waiter's cloth, its little beard
lost in the white pipes of a wide collar.
More disturbing than the collar—
a kind of Tudor ruff—is its execution.
There's no evidence of lace,
and the pleat mouths opened
down the side turned toward us
gape abjectly, only to be filled,
stoppered, near the middle,
with but the merest nod to perspective.
For a people so accustomed to beheadings,
one of the joys of ruffs must have been
the challenge of rendering their recesses—
such apertures, opened like a throat.
Hence, the sitter's slight turn, facilitating
the peek inside.
            Who painted this monkey,
or how, is not the point. It was "produced."
It was sold, unsigned, for the purposes
of tasteful "interior design." It will do
as it's told and tells its owners
and their friends what they already know
about mastery and a misty bygone era,
that hard curve of holes grasped
without thought, molded as for the hand.

The Waiter

Angel of Death, in your transforming hands
the straw we lie on turns to softest down
Baudelaire

Drawing out a giddy exchange to divert her from my protests
that she needed to go to the hospital, death or death's best server
    sat my mother outside (it was a warm night) so she could people-watch,
    and bowed and groveled, flirted and joked, everything my father never did,
and hers, only too well. She only ever wanted to feel special.
    I knew because It was my specialty. But at some point there was a misstep,

a transition I couldn't make—from tone to pitch, say, or algebra to probability.
Something happened—or things—or didn't. I hit a wall, I became someone bad
    at waiting. Forgetting the order, I dropped the tray and soiled my shoes,
    a burst appendix, a Judas keeled over in his field. So, cowering in the doorway
while she lay in bed deteriorating those twenty years later, I recognized the skill
    that makes you feel like you're the only one. In her delirium,

she was an easy target, a tipsy, stood-up date. He was the antithesis
of the waiter who ignored them, my young parents, in Paris—
    my mother tracking him around the room, determined to use her French,
    that there must be a misunderstanding, my father's grim smirk bumpkinish
in the corner of her eye, hunched over his elbows, his short neck
    jammed down so his head was square with his shoulders.

How is it that we come so far from where we wanted to be? Humankind
cannot bear to be cheated of our most guarded truths, to be out-served, to stand by
    while death works his magic. At every turn culture combats it. To say I was taken
    off-guard or lost in the catacombs of her unhappiness—or more to the point,
that I'd already lost her, that I was alone, twenty-three—these are just things I say.
    The waiter snaps his cloth, backs into shadow. The punishment is unmitigable.

Italian Suit

Where is it now? that purple suit she found
in a storefront along the lane
to Santa Maria in Trastevere,
the suit my mother visited each day,
until, at last, she splurged, bringing it
back with her over the ocean
royal as Mrs. Lowell's coffin.
And surely she wore it
a few times before it would hang
bodiless, unoccasioned in her closet—
the sharp lines the flair
loud for Birmingham or Atlanta.
—No, she wore it, I remember,
her last Easter at my cousin's,
blazing betrayed because she'd only come
out of propriety, because I said I would,—
but when I finally turned up,
booze-puffy and twenty, she was through.
So I made my Bloody and said fine,
you want to be like that.

Stranded there, was she thinking of Italy,
the apse's mosaic
we stood beneath with our Cokes
burning down our throats,
Jesus abstract and pitiless,
his gold book? Where is the suit
that crossed the ocean, was worn and abandoned
by her body? Off what sharp shoulders,
in which consignment shop,
pressed between dull powers,
what hidden glory?

Nuclear Medicine

Weekdays I wheeled the vial
across the hospital,
its fifty-pound lead drum
blowing through the atrium
where sky crashed in
on potted trees, and workmen
were walling up the old
ER entrance where I'd rolled
in my mother, deteriorating,
slumped. No more waiting
room delirium and panic
now. Watching the clock,
I had three minutes to get
the radioactive agent
to its subject, one of a set
of identical twins,
so his heart could betray
its damage. No time to see
that wall close up like the artery
that killed my mother, or the one
that would darken a section
of the vet's heart muscle.
I took the tunnel
under Clifton Road, the decay drum
catching momentum
down the ramp as I cried out
to strangers, *organ transplant,*
coming through—some white lie
to clear the way,
not thinking of the beating bag
I'd dreamed of carrying
her heart in, or how being
alone with her dying
left me exposed,

as to a naked dose.
Lying on the scanner bed
in his room of lead,
some Don or Ron, Harry or Larry
was prepped for my delivery.
Not thinking how personal,
how molecular, upheaval
gets inside us. Riddling
the body, the body releasing
that which hurts
yet preserves us—what stress
damages the heart,
what we can measure of it.

Lookout Mountain

As you drive down the valley, Lookout Mountain
crests, a green wall-wave gathering you
into the fact of her death: the cemetery
tucked under the bluff, the plaque's precision
blocked in caps, a neatness to it all
she might have liked. And maybe this
is why you're brushing off ants, ripping grass
the mower missed, or winding a stray
whip of weed-eater cable around your fist.
Good steward, good son, you were a good son.
Now let the lines unravel, let her name
survive its saying. A motorcade
passes, graves reflected down the long
hearse window. You're already someone else.

Upon the much lamented decease of my mother,
Susan Clap Freeman

Anagram:

A Falcon Swoops Near Me

A falcon swoops near me.
The falcon cannot hear me,
hearing nothing else
but her ankle bells.
Each pass she passes close enough to raise
the hair on my arm.
I raise my arm
to the wing-beaten stars.

I'm Practicing Dance Moves

I'm practicing dance moves in the hallway
of Emory University hospital, Radiation Wing,
not that I have cancer, that I know of,
I just work here. I'm twenty-four, hungover,
a secretary imagining my dance instructor,
Victor, at the studio mirror. I'm practicing
leading with my left, rocking fore and aft,
and off the hip, pulling in a twist
like I did diving as a kid.
Back here they haven't mopped yet,
I steady my spot on the wall,
a radiation sign's yellow and black relief.
A half-life below, the cyclotron spins
sugar to an unstable valence—
change, which, though you can't
pinpoint it, pinpoints change.
This being research, I'm mostly alone,
clapping the soft three on four, though one
or two doctors must have seen me swivel.
My mother, who got me this job, is a year
dead, I am as one who raises his forehead
from the bat-end of grief and lunges off.
In sympathy, my roommates brought me out
to Latin night, one brought Victor home.
His heels scored the kitchen floor with spirals
I walked like a pilgrim in the morning.
One hand raised for your hand,
the other reaching for your shoulder-blade,
I open out and leading you across
my body, turn and follow, turning you.

Trastevere

Oh, sometimes I get a good feeling, yeah…
Etta James

—And I can see clear across the Tiber, I can take
any of seven ancient bridges to Trastevere
where my mother's wearing purple—not the funereal
purple of flowers, or the purple veins flowering
to the surface of the skin of the dying, her dying—
but the suit she found the rare
Italian nerve to finally buy
after a week wandering the loose-end streets
sprouting off the square.
                    And in the market
where it doesn't matter if I'm underage
she endows me with the secret of Wild Turkey,
oh, wildly underestimated. And later
we'll go looking for that restaurant as shops roll shut
and old men fiddle with scooters by lamplight,
their radios throating soccer games, staccato.
And our feet are light
over cobblestone made
from volcanic ash—blasted, blanketing,
hardened in the hills; stones, which,
they say, come summer (only a month or so away),
give under the pressure of heels.

The End of Analysis

At the end of analysis you should face your analyst.
It's recommended that you enjoy a lengthy goodbye.
You've spent a long time together.
After years pinned to that couch, staring at that painting,
the old man of the sea will yield his true form.
For example: a slender gay man in his late thirties,
clean-smelling and bald, his anonymous sky-blue tie
and fitted slacks, like a holidaying uncle
in a French Impressionist painting, except
instead of the Rhine it's the Ohio.
The spell is broken. You can see him now—
around town, maybe, or driving home behind you
in his Honda Civic, which he's always done,
but which you've never noticed.
Imagine you've entered the painting.
It's midnight, you've got him pinned. His colony of seals
sleep piled like slipper shells. You can ask him anything.
He's no longer slippery. *Who am I? Can I love? Am I real?*
The hero's question is always what's holding me back.
It implies something went wrong and can be made right.
That the past continues to operate, that there is disorder.
And that there is disorder is predicated upon a prior state
of greater order. Once he commented on your slovenly appearance.
Once you went back for something. A question maybe.
You knocked. A no-no. He wasn't all yours.
Having seen your old man in you, having seen you weren't all hers,
your mother asked and asked, what happened to the old you?
I don't know, you'd say, squirming away. Or, nothing.
What happened to your mother? the physician on call after hours
working on her asked wearily, befuddled from behind his glasses.
Knowledge and propitiation are demanded of the hero.
Where are you getting this? Your Latin teacher?
What about you? your analyst asked. Maybe you're in love with me.
Suppose you were supposed to say no. What happened

to the old you? She didn't mean you, maybe, so much as herself.
The one she wanted back. The one you never knew.
Is that what you went back for? Because nobody ever told you?
Your mother's very sick, the physician on call had said.
Meaning dead. You gave it till the end of the week.

Venus in Transit

Pearl month, midsummer, the north inclines
unto its star. Sugars in the peach
are knit in self-forgetful concentration.
The estrogen molecule sails through the blood,
shaped, in the *Scientific American*,
like Botticelli's shell. At the top of the stairwell
to the observatory, a collie's sprawled
under a table, out of the dome's
searching slat of sun—*For to withstand
her look I am not able* goes the old poem.
You stand on a crate, looking not up,
but down into the eyepiece. The simmering
disc is the sun. You're looking for a kernel
intervening, Lucifer wending
among the worlds, a merchant-adventurer
flagged, for the balance of six hours
out of hundreds of years, in the doldrums.
Morning star and evening, spotted now
in the middle of the year, of day, day's dark
roving pupil, no star, demoted to the wanderer
you are, spot of time, spot on the liver or lungs.

Björklunden

The beams of our house are cedar, and our rafters of fir
Song of Songs

The name translates to birch grove, though cedars,
ropey, creaking, growing right up to the water,
predominate, clinging tight
to rocks that come up with them.
Hearty but short-lived,
what birches there are are bare,
peach-tinged or beige against the snow.
A clutch of four outside my window wags
their tatters, dark eyes unblinking,
watching for the fortunate isles.

In Door County it's hard
not to think of an open door.

Lakeside, the cobbles' gray clatter.
A wing's feathers and bones
look mown in their wet arrangement,
three quills loosed suggestively from their row.
The skull's cocked over to the side
(lacunae that were the eyes),
vertebrae twisting after it
like tiny, articulated anvils.
The breastbone's arch, the delicate jaw tines
spongiform behind the beak, chipped,
bleached, the keratin eaten away.
Everywhere the cedar needles'
little blood-brown chicken feet.
A wisp of feather combed over the greening pate.

In Door County it's hard not to think
of a door opening.

Long and low, the meltwater waves
sluice through ankle-deep ice that seems
dumped out from champagne buckets.
Long and low and gray-green (perhaps the tide is coming in),
like beater bars pushing back the weft,
they slap back low beneath the shelf,
touching the hem and clearing out,
running blind fingers over the bedrock's pitted braille.

in memory of Claudia Emerson

A Pelican of the Wilderness

APPLETON, WI

Between bends in the river, you can hear
the ice elbow for room.
Out in the middle the mind can't believe
it isn't moving, imagines movement.
I pick my way down trestle boards
to see what it is that's out there. Not a volleyball,
or a thatched white basket. But a straggler
pelican. Facing south. Frozen.
Her companions are in Florida.
Like an old pet left behind,
she wasn't going to make the trip.

I remember the tall porcelain swan
in a neighbor's house I went inside just the once
to tell her I was afraid my mother wasn't coming back
from her long morning walk (I was always measuring
how long she'd been gone, how long she had left).
Once, she almost froze, slipping on her long morning walk
in freak Alabama ice.

Have you heard what they say about the pelican in her piety?
Her starvelings nursed on blood
pecked from her own breast?
Justice and sacrifice—so many big ideas
seem to end in ice.
In Florida, the martyrs thaw,
a kind of heaven to some.
But me, I like the cold.

Long-wave red light dredges the treetops.
Satiny steam monologues downriver,
talking a pink, then pewter-blue streak.
Engorged like a gular pouch,
the moon looks down from the height of its sanctuary.

Door to Remain

WHIDBEY ISLAND, WA

A shipment of mist is coming in from Japan,
rain ground to grist, blotting out the mountains,
lightning pushing pins into a pincushion.
An outlet to open ocean has warped the windward firs,
wind barreling unobstructed down the strait,
blindsiding the island as if the Sound's
Eustachian tube were stuck open, as in the ear
of an anorexic tortured by the white noise between worlds,
inner and outer. This door to remain unlocked
during business hours, signs on the mainland read.
God's tenseless infinitive, wielded as imperative.

Letter to Quinn from Provincetown

Love of my twenties, we never even kissed.
Remember when you snatched the straw hat
off my head? You were in the back of a truck,
driving off at dusk. Going later to retrieve it,
I found you sleepy drunk, burning popcorn.
Muse of my first published poem, Quinn on the phone
in the Arkansas rain, did I ever tell you the story
of that hat? I'd gone to find my mother's grave,
and pinched it from the men's room moonlighting,
best as I could tell, as a costume closet.
Yet who has not embraced a skeleton?
Baudelaire asks. *What does the costume matter?*
I'm writing this in the yard in Provincetown.
When the sun hits the house, I sit out here and read
and drink my coffee. It's December 23rd,
I can see my breath…There was that night
in Jacob's attic (I guess we climbed his ladder),
the stultifying air where nothing happened.
Might-have-been-Quinn, it seems it never could.
There was P, my brother, H, my girlfriends,
and now D, who I myself became
enamored of that day at the waterfall
before that hot and bothered, sleepless attic night—
how he undressed so casually to swim.
How elegantly he rolled his cigarettes.
I got him to myself on the ride home.
We sang a mix tape's half-step modulations.
Now y'all have kids and a house, and I don't need
to ask—happiness. P would say,
and my mother, too, that it was destined,
that you're charmed, or, in my mother's parlance,
have a halo (needless to say,
she didn't think she had one)—like a straw hat,
or your red-gold hair, lifted from an angel.

Once you swung through—to fly out?—
and we caught a movie. I had my motorcycle.
It was batshit crazy, the movie. When the credits
went up, you turned to me—I don't know—
to kiss? I guess I'll go on thinking so.
Visitors have stopped by to see the house.
The clean white walls and loving carpentry
I enjoy all the more—like food
cooked by someone else—because
unlike Thoreau I didn't make it.
Borrowed space and time, and art
more found than made…Is it because,
as Larkin says, we all hate home
and having to be there that I can't make one?
Poets are creatures of the in-between:
we live parallel to, not in, this world,
and can't quite make another.
Or maybe I was afraid, starving myself,
like my mother, of pleasure I didn't deserve,
or couldn't afford to have denied me.
I could go on with the close calls:
when you split with H and invited me
in his stead—to New Orleans?
What if I'd gone? Probably bad
in the long run. With some immediate
good. Or lots, who knows. Or B's wedding,
my Lazaran hangover. What if you'd been
my date? You should have! we'll forever say.
Cool Quinn, charmed darling, is it beauty
or desire or insecurity that leaves me wrecked
at the end of the night, of the year?
It's hard to uncathect; it feeds on distance,
unbridgeable ridges, friend groups ranked
around us stubborn as suburbs.
Yet by whim or visit or invitation,
by music festival or underclassman

crush, you're planted deep in the plot
where one life ended and another struggles to begin.
In fertile ground, even if I'm no husband.

Northern Gannet

PROVINCETOWN, MA

One great wing, splayed
as if for a midair maneuver,
or rowing into the depths,
was festooned with seaweed,
cassette tape unwound.
Its masked eyes and eye-
lined features gave it a mystic
and at once almost muppetish look.
Overlooking the beak,
I thought it might be an osprey.
I'd seen gannets dive
(not knowing the name)
a hundred yards out.
On YouTube they arrow-shower,
bullet-trailing sixty feet deep
when sardines sound.
Its soft-toned, almost haloish
cantaloupe head feathers
were faded, mussed.
The sun was setting. That far down,
the rentals were boarded up:
the Crow's Nest, the Double Dip.
The gannet's apartment
is on the side of a cliff.
His neighbors live all around him.
The tide peeled back, as if
in a reverential withdrawal
before the wind. Towards town,
picture windows lit up
wood beams, hanging pots.
Winda, I wrote as a child,
sounding it out the way

my mother said it.
Only later, with the sun down,
winding the rich, quiet
streets (she liked it better
where people were—even just,
like an edge of moon,
looking in) did I think of her
crumpled body I refused
to see once there was nothing
more the doctors could do.
I told myself she wouldn't have
wanted me to, as she hadn't
wanted me to call an ambulance,
hadn't wanted to make a fuss.
Call it closure, then,
when the gannet narrows
its area of impact behind
the spear point of its beak,
when I cinched my jacket,
and feeling for my gloves and hat,
just to know they were there,
owned the grateful echo
of my boots, the harborside light
that would hold another minute.

April doet wat hij wil is a Dutch proverb that means that April weather does whatever it wants

The epigraph is from a New England Puritan anagram elegy for John Cotton ("O Honie Knott") by John Fisk (1652)

"Meet the Beatles": the title of a Beatles album (1964); see John Murillo's "Ode to the Crossfader" (*Up Jump the Boogie*, 2010); snips from the Beatles song "I Wanna Hold Your Hand"; "John" in the poem is John Lennon

"Preamble": "anesthetizing the patient": see the beginning of T.S. Eliot's "The Love Song of J. Alfred Prufrock" (1915); "acute...vanishing": see Wallace Stevens, "The Idea of Order at Key West" (1934)

"The Alabama Theater": references the silent movie *The Phantom of the Opera* (1925)

"Doormat": references John Donne's "Holy Sonnet XIV" (1633)

"The Shirelles": snips from the Shirelles song "Everybody Loves a Lover" (1962)

"Cold Sweat" is a James Brown song title (1967)

"Montevallo": riffs on Emily Dickinson's (1830-1886) "A Bird, came down the Walk"

"Vestavia": references David and Goliath, Michelangelo's statue *David* (1504), in particular

"Majestic Diner": alludes to George Herbert's "Mattens" and "The Star" (1633), which my poem quotes ("Glitter, and curl, and wind..."); "going all along" is from Dickinson's "Some keep the Sabbath going to Church"; references the lyrics and music video of Michael Jackson's "Thriller" (1982), as well as the cover of the eponymous album; the last section cribs from Frank Bidart's "Love Incarnate" (1997), a take on Dante's *La Vita Nuova* (1294)

"The Waiter": the epigraph is from Charles Baudelaire's "La Mort des pauvres" (1857), Richard Howard trans.; the "Humankind" part is a mix of Eliot's famous lines from "Burnt Norton" (1935) and Plato's *The Republic* (375 BCE?), *382b*

"A Falcon Swoops Near Me": in the style of a 17th century New England anagram elegy; riffs on W.B. Yeats's poem "The Second Coming" (1920)

"Venus in Transit": the "old poem" referenced and quoted is Thomas Wyatt's (1503-1542) "Some fowls there be that have so perfect sight"

"Björklunden": echoes *The Tempest* (1610/11?): "Those are pearls that were his eyes…" "The 'long and low' rhetoric echoes the end of Elizabeth Bishop's 'At the Fishhouses' (1948)"

"A Pelican of the Wilderness": see Psalm 102; "The Pelican in Her Piety" is a Christian-adopted myth about mother pelicans "vulning," or wounding themselves to nurse their young on blood in times of distress

"Letter to Quinn from Provincetown": see Baudelaire's "Danse macabre" (1861), Richard Howard trans.; the Larkin quote is from "Poetry of Departures" (1954); the "Cool Quinn…" sentence borrows rhythm and syntax from Melissa Range's poem "Lampblack" (*Scriptorium*, 2016)

"Northern Gannet": "reverential withdrawing" is Emerson (*Nature*, 1836); the italicized lines are cribbed from a children's book called *Water Birds* (1955); my ending echoes the end of Whittier's "Snow-Bound: A Winter Idyl" (1866): "The traveller owns the grateful sense / Of sweetness near…"

ACKNOWLEDGMENTS

Thank you to the editors of the following publications in which versions of these poems appeared:

Birmingham Poetry Review: "Lookout Mountain," "Björklunden," "Meet the Beatles"
Blackbird: "My Mother's Morning Walks"
Cumberland River Review: "Wyeth"
Ecotone: "Shades Creek, Panther Sighting," "Gum"
Grist: "Venus in Transit"
New England Review: "Trastevere"
Poetry Magazine: "Across the Street"
Poetry Northwest: "The Shirelles"
Saint Katherine Review: "Italian Suit," "A Falcon Swoops Near Me"
Southern Humanities Review: "Majestic Diner," "Door to Remain"
Southwest Review: "Vestavia"
Spoon River Poetry Review: "Doormat"
The Threepenny Review: "I'm Practicing Dance Moves"
TriQuarterly: "Cold Sweat"
Valparaiso Poetry Review: "Montevallo"
The Yale Review: "Nuclear Medicine"

Thanks to all my writing teachers, starting with my mom.

Thanks to Broki for twenty years of friendship and poetic guidance.

Thanks to my grad school teachers, including Beth Gylys, Leon Stokesbury, David Bottoms, Scott Cairns, Cornelius Eady, Alex Socarides, and Frances Dickey.

Thanks to my family for suffering my obsessions and disclosures, especially Dad, my brother, Stuart, my twin sister, Chamberlain, and my godparents, Lynne and Tom.

Thanks to all my fellow workshoppers and readers, especially Sara Martin, Laura Neal, Gabe Kruis, Philip Matthews, Kannan Mahadevan, Rose McLarney, Thomas Kane, Katy Didden, Claire McQuerry, Andrew McSorley, Danny Ceballos, Meredith Mason, Jake Adam York, James Davis May, James Thomas Miller, Emily Schulten, Eric Nelson, John A. Nieves, Rachel Marie Patterson, Laura Scheffler Morgan, Tryfon Tolides, Pilar Gómez Ibáñez, Adrienne Su, Amy Newman, David Rivard, Richie Hofmann, Elizabeth Quinn, Kimberly Johnson, and Tom Sleigh.

Thanks to the Fine Arts Work Center in Provincetown, the Hambidge Center for the Arts, the Ucross Foundation, and to Lynne Rudder Baker for generous support to help me write this book.

Thanks to John Poch for believing in this book and for your comments.

Thanks to Karl Kirchwey for picking this book, writing such nice things about it, and for your comments.

Finally, thanks to Ranger for your spirit, integrity, genius, generosity, and love.